Tomorrow's Geography

for Edexcel GCSE Specification A

REVISION GUIDE

Unit 1 Geographical Skills and Challenges

Steph Warren

The Publishers would like to thank the following for permission to reproduce copyright material:

Photo credits: **page 2** *t* © Steph Warren; **page 3** imagery copyright Getmapping plc/supplied by Skyscan.co.uk; **page 13** © Steph Warren; **page 14** reproduced from Ordnance Survey mapping with permission of the Controller of HMSO. © Crown copyright. All rights reserved. Licence number 100036470; **page 28** © Steph Warren; **page 29** *tb* © Steph Warren; **page 34** © Steph Warren; **page 35** *tb* © Steph Warren; **page 37** *b* © Art Photo Picture/Fotolia.com; **page 38** *t* © Patrick Hermans/Fotolia.com, *b* © Steph Warren; **page 39** *all* © Steph Warren, except *tl* © Peiro Tonin/www.CartoonStock.com.

Every effort has been made to trace all copyright holders, but if any have been inadvertently overlooked the Publishers will be pleased to make the necessary arrangements at the first opportunity.

Although every effort has been made to ensure that website addresses are correct at time of going to press, Hodder Education cannot be held responsible for the content of any website mentioned in this book. It is sometimes possible to find a relocated web page by typing in the address of the home page for a website in the URL window of your browser.

Hachette UK's policy is to use papers that are natural, renewable and recyclable products and made from wood grown in sustainable forests. The logging and manufacturing processes are expected to conform to the environmental regulations of the country of origin.

Orders: please contact Bookpoint Ltd, 130 Milton Park, Abingdon, Oxon OX14 4SB. Telephone: (44) 01235 827720. Fax: (44) 01235 400454. Lines are open 9.00–5.00, Monday to Saturday, with a 24-hour message answering service. Visit our website at www.hoddereducation.co.uk

© Steph Warren 2011
First published in 2011 by
Hodder Education,
An Hachette UK Company
338 Euston Road
London NW1 3BH

Impression number   5 4 3 2 1
Year   2016 2015 2014 2013 2012

Cover image: © Skyscan/J Farmer
Illustrations by Countryside Illustrations and Gray Publishing
Produced and typeset in 11/13pt Myriad by Gray Publishing, Tunbridge Wells, Kent
Printed in Spain

A catalogue record for this title is available from the British Library

ISBN: 978 1444 11533 8

Contents

Introduction

This unit contains two sections:

- Section A – Geographical Skills.
- Section B – Challenges for the Planet.

All questions in both sections must be attempted; there is no choice on this unit.

Section A includes the following topics:

- Basic skills.
- Cartographic skills.
- Graphical skills.
- Geographical enquiry skills.
- ICT skills.
- Geographical Information Systems (GIS) skills.

Section B includes the following topics:

- The causes, effects and responses to climate change.
- Sustainable development for the planet.

Exam Tips

- The examination lasts for one hour and the paper has four questions. Questions 1 and 2 cover Section A and Questions 3 and 4 cover Section B. Both sections have 25 marks allocated to them; hence a total of 50 marks are available on this paper.
- Section A usually has more marks allocated to Question 1, which is the map-work question, than Question 2, which covers the other topics. In Section B the marks are usually fairly equally distributed between the two questions.
- There will always be an Ordnance Survey (OS) map with this paper from the Landranger 1:50,000 series. A key will always be provided so that the map symbols do not need to be learned, but you should be familiar with maps showing different types of land use and landforms. There will also be various photographs and other resources.
- There will be a variety of question types such as short answer, cartographic, graphical and extended answer.
- **Foundation Tier** – This paper will include multiple-choice and gap-fill questions. These will not appear on the Higher Tier paper.
- **Foundation and Higher Tier** – A 6-mark question will appear on both tier papers. It will usually be the last question on the paper and will be levels marked.

ZNANIYE FOUNDATION

FREE
EALING
KIDS
ACTIVITIES

AGES 5+

WEEKLY SESSIONS

20 YEARS EXPERIENCE

What parents and carers say:

"Inclusive and relaxed atmosphere"

"Those running the club offer the most personal and individual approach"

"Creative, interactive and full of energy!"

SATURDAY CLUB
SATURDAYS 10.30 – 13.40

MATHS SESSIONS
SATURDAYS 10.00 – 14.00

HOLIDAY CAMPS
CHRISTMAS, EASTER AND SUMMER

CINEMA CLUB
TUESDAYS FORTNIGHTLY

WWW.ZNANIYEFOUNDATION.CO.UK/EVENTS
CONTACT@ZNANIYEFOUNDATION.CO.UK
07545325930
@ZNANIYEFOUNDATION

Hi, we're Znaniye Foundation!

We offer a range of activities and services for the children and families of Ealing to ensure that all children are being given access to academic support and progress opportunities, as well as the chance to increase and maintain their overall well-being.

Our 3 Main Programmes:

Saturday Club

Welcoming kids aged 5+ for a wide variety of free activities that change each week, including Arts and Crafts, Music, Drama, Sports, Educational Support and more. We focus on improving and maintaining mental and physical wellbeing.

Holiday Camps

Free Day Camps each Half Term and School Holiday that ensures local children on Free School Meals can access safe spaces, a healthy fresh meal, as well as activities and exercise whilst out of school.

English, Maths and Science

We offer English, Maths and Science starting at Age 5, all the way up to A Level. These are offered at various locations across Ealing Borough each week, and are free of charge.

1 Basic Skills

How to label and annotate diagrams, graphs, sketch maps

You could be asked to do this in any of the units. For example, in Unit 2 you might get this question: draw an annotated diagram showing the formation of a waterfall or stack.

On the Unit 1 exam, you could be asked to:

● complete the annotations on a diagram
● label a graph to show its main features
● annotate a sketch.

Exam Tip

What is the difference between a label and an annotation?

● A label is a simple descriptive point.
● An annotation is a label with more detailed description or an explanatory point.

Exam Tips

Ensure you have practice looking at Ordnance Survey (OS) maps and photographs of the same area so that you can identify:

● features on the map that aren't on the photograph
● features on the photograph that aren't on the map.

ACTIVITIES

1 Name one feature that is on Figure 1 (on page 2) but is not on the map on page 14.
2 Name one feature that is on the map on page 14 but is not on Figure 1.

How to draw, label and annotate sketches

For the exam you will usually need to show that you are able to complete a sketch. It is unlikely you would be asked to draw the whole sketch because of time constraints.

Exam Tips

Follow the simple rules below:

● Some of the most important lines such as rivers, coastline and the outline of the hills will have been drawn for you. You could be asked to complete them.
● You could then be asked to add certain features such as woodlands, settlements or roads.
● You may possibly then be asked to label and annotate your sketch.

Figure 1 A photograph of Buttermere

Figure 2 An incomplete sketch map of Buttermere

ACTIVITY

Figure 2 is an incomplete sketch of Figure 1. Copy out and then complete the sketch by adding the rest of the hills, Buttermere Lake, the field pattern and Buttermere Village.

How to interpret aerial, oblique and satellite photographs

Photographs show features of the landscape that are not on OS maps, such as the crops being grown in the fields. You might be asked to interpret aerial, oblique or satellite photographs, but do you know the difference?

- **Aerial** photographs are taken directly above, like the view of a flying bird.
- **Oblique** photographs are taken at an angle, so that the details of buildings can be seen.
- **Satellite** photographs are images taken from space. They show patterns of features such as street lights in an urban area. Although they can show much more detail such as cars on a street.

When a photograph is interpreted, it involves describing and explaining the physical and human geography which can be seen on the photograph. It is important when interpreting photographs that the writing is coherent and shows good literacy skills in expressing geographical points.

Figure 3

ACTIVITIES

1 Is Figure 3 an aerial, oblique or satellite image?
2 A village can be seen on the photograph. Describe the shape of the village.
3 What services might be in the village which cannot be seen on the photograph, but would be marked on an OS map?
4 Describe the landscape shown on the photograph.
5 Describe the land use shown on the photograph.

Exam Tip

You might be asked whether a photograph is an oblique, aerial or satellite image.

Atlas maps

How to describe the distribution or pattern of physical or human features on an atlas map

Atlases contain maps that show physical patterns such as the height of the land and human patterns such as population density. Atlas maps can be at different scales, showing features in a country through to global features.

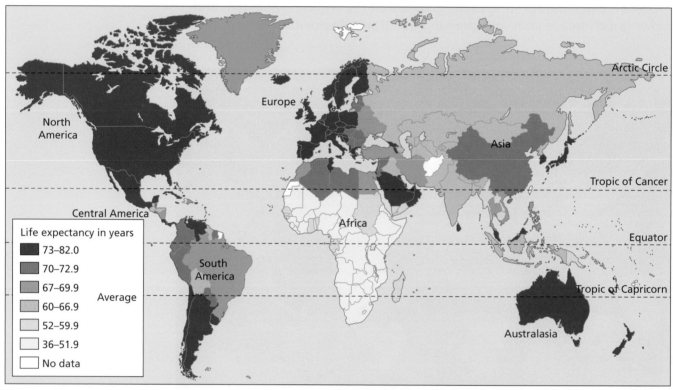

Figure 1 Life expectancy in 2003

In an exam you will need to be able to describe patterns of human geography and patterns of physical geography and relate them to each other.

When describing a distribution or pattern on an atlas map:
- start with a general statement about where the features are located on the map
- then go into greater detail such as mentioning the area of the country or any particular features such as the name of the sea next to that area
- it is a good idea to point out any anomalies.

Describe the distribution of life expectancy shown in Figure 1.   (4 marks)

Life expectancy is high in North America, Australia, Western Europe and parts of South America.

Life expectancy is low (36–51.9 years) in central and southern Africa. It is also below average in parts of Central America which is surprising as all of the other countries in that area are above average.

Brazil's life expectancy is one of the lowest in South America.

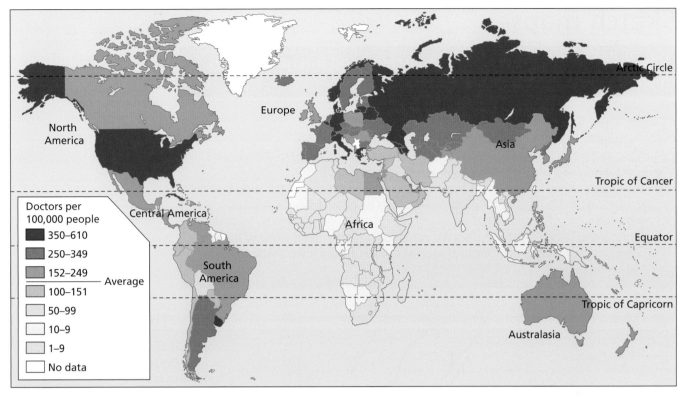

Figure 2 Number of doctors per 100,000 people in 2004

ACTIVITIES

1 Describe the pattern shown in Figure 2.
2 Compare and contrast the information on Figures 1 and 2.

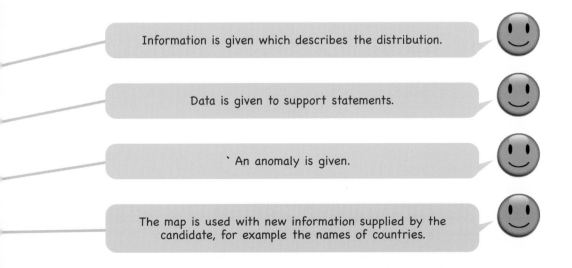

Sketch maps

How to draw, label, annotate, understand and interpret sketch maps

Exam Tips

- In the exam you usually will be completing sketch maps.
- Remember, the examiner is not looking for a perfect replica of the map but accuracy with the location of roads, woodlands or other features will be expected.
- If you are asked to complete a sketch map, but not instructed what to include, just include the important features such as roads, railway lines, settlements and woods.

ACTIVITIES

Copy out and complete the sketch map in Figure 3. Add the following features:

- Crummock Water, Loweswater and the river connecting them.
- B5289 and the rest of the secondary road network.
- A mixed wood.
- A caravan site and a camp and caravan site.
- National/regional cycle network.
- Three car parks.
- 100-metre contour line.

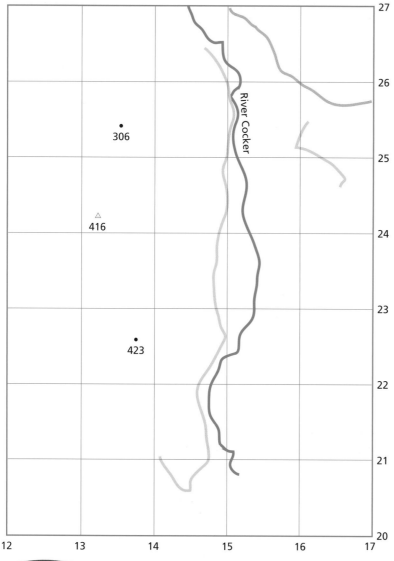

Figure 3 A sketch map of Lorton Vale. 2 cm = 1 km

Exam Tips

- In the exam it is best to use a pencil or black pen to complete the sketch map.
- Use different types of lines such as dashed or dots to show different features.
- Don't forget to provide a key!

Ordnance Survey (OS) maps

Map skills

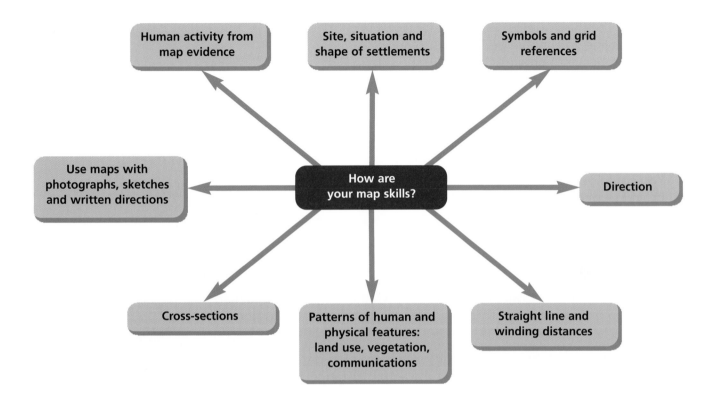

Figure 4 How are your map skills?

Figure 4 contains many map skills. You need to be competent in a lot of map skills, many of which may not appear in the exam paper, but you never know.

Symbols, four- and six-figure grid references

Do I need to learn the symbols?

Many symbols provide a 'clue' to what they represent, for example, a blue P is car parking. Symbols will always be provided in a key with the 50,000 OS map, so you don't need to remember them. If you can learn some of them it will save you time in not having to look them up.

Remember if you are asked to complete sketch maps use the correct symbols from the key.

Which grid references should I be able to do?

You are required to be able to do both four- and six-figure grid references.

Remember, to find the grid reference 218405:

- Always go along and then up (see Figure 5).
- The first two numbers (21) provide the line you require, the third number (8) is how far towards the next line you should go. The fourth and fifth numbers (40) provide the line up the side that you require, the sixth number (5) is how far towards the next line you should go.

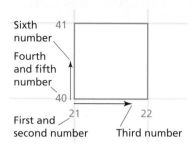

Figure 5 How to use a map's grid reference

Compass directions

- These are normally used with the OS map.
- You could be asked to orientate a photograph with the map and then provide a direction for a feature.
- Remember: north will be taken as the top of the map following the grid lines.

Straight line and winding distances

You may be asked to measure the distance between two points on a map along a road or a railway line. This could be a straight line or a winding distance:

- To measure a straight line, use a ruler or a piece of paper. Don't forget to use the scale line on the map to get the actual distance on the ground.
- To measure a winding distance, split the route into a number of straight sections. Then add up these distances and use the scale line to find out the distance on the ground.

ACTIVITY

Measure the length of the B5289 on the OS map extract (see page 14).

Exam Tip

It is useful to have a piece of string in the exam to measure distances. (Long hair can be an advantage here!)

Exam Tips

- You may also be asked to estimate the area of a feature. For example, the area of Loweswater on the OS map extract.
- Try to imagine whole grid squares. If you add the pieces of Loweswater not in 1221 in your mind to that grid square it would almost fill it.
- Therefore, the area of Loweswater is 1 km^2 as that is the size of a grid square.

Exam Tip

It is useful to remember that the distance between grid lines on a 1:50,000 map (these are the only ones used on exam papers) is 2 cm which is 1 km on the ground.

Cross-sections

Cross-sections show how relief varies along a chosen line on the map. A cross-section is drawn as a graph which shows distance along the *x*-axis (horizontal) and height on the *y*-axis (vertical). The scale must be chosen carefully so that a true representation of the area is produced.

In the exam it is unlikely that you would be asked to draw a cross-section but you may be asked to complete and/or annotate one. You should also be able to interpret cross-sections:

- If the land is steep, the contours will be close together.
- If the contours are far apart, the land is gently sloping.
- An absence of contours indicates flat land.

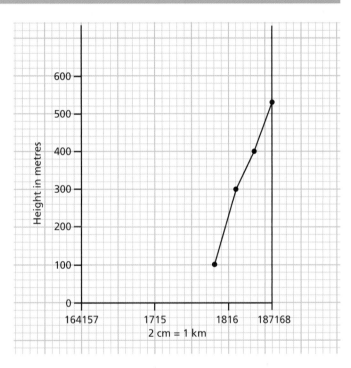

Figure 6 An incomplete cross-section

ACTIVITIES

Figure 6 shows an incomplete cross-section between spot height 641 at grid reference 164157 to spot height 526 at grid reference 187168 (see the OS map on page 14).

1 Complete the cross-section.
2 Mark the following on your cross-section (label with an arrow and use a suitable key):
   - an area of deciduous woodland
   - an area of coniferous woodland
   - the B5289
   - Buttermere Lake.
3 What does your cross-section show you about the relief and land use of the area?

Patterns of human and physical features

There are a number of physical and human features which you could be asked to recognise on OS maps and to describe the patterns that they produce.

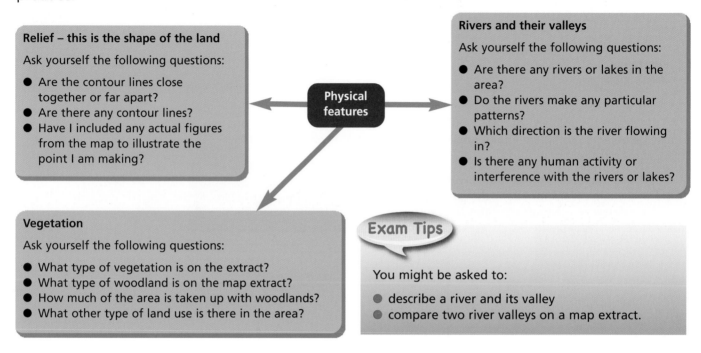

Relief – this is the shape of the land

Ask yourself the following questions:

- Are the contour lines close together or far apart?
- Are there any contour lines?
- Have I included any actual figures from the map to illustrate the point I am making?

Physical features

Rivers and their valleys

Ask yourself the following questions:

- Are there any rivers or lakes in the area?
- Do the rivers make any particular patterns?
- Which direction is the river flowing in?
- Is there any human activity or interference with the rivers or lakes?

Vegetation

Ask yourself the following questions:

- What type of vegetation is on the extract?
- What type of woodland is on the map extract?
- How much of the area is taken up with woodlands?
- What other type of land use is there in the area?

Exam Tips

You might be asked to:

- describe a river and its valley
- compare two river valleys on a map extract.

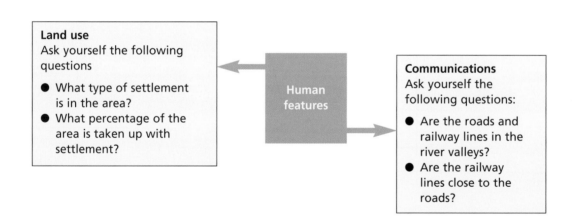

Land use
Ask yourself the following questions

- What type of settlement is in the area?
- What percentage of the area is taken up with settlement?

Human features

Communications
Ask yourself the following questions:

- Are the roads and railway lines in the river valleys?
- Are the railway lines close to the roads?

Exam Tips

When describing a distribution:

- Start with a general statement about where the features are located on the map.
- Then go into greater detail such as mentioning grid references of where features are located.
- State how much of the map is taken up by the feature.
- If describing woodland, what type of woodland is on the map?
- Point out any anomalies.
- Remember, if you are asked to describe the distribution of settlement on a map, do not discuss individual settlement shapes.

ACTIVITY

Describe the pattern of woodland on the map on page 14.

The site, situation and shape of settlements

Site

You need to be able to describe the site and situation of settlements on a map. In order to describe or identify the site of a settlement there are certain human and physical features that you need to remember.

An easy way to remember is using the acronym: **SHAWL**. Do you know what the letters stand for?

Site factors
S   shelter from strong winds and storms
H   height above sea level
A   aspect – the way that the slope faces
W   water supply
L   land that the settlement is built on such as above the floodplain, fertile land, type of slope

Situation

The situation of a settlement is its position in relation to its surroundings. When you are describing the situation of a settlement on an OS map, you should describe the human and physical features around it. Try to remember the acronym: **PARC**.

Situation factors
P   places
A   accessibility
R   relief
C   communications

Exam Tip

You could be asked to explain the site of a settlement using an OS map and a photograph.

Shape

The shape of the settlement is the pattern that it makes. This refers to the way that the buildings are arranged. Settlement shape is concentrated usually on villages.

ACTIVITIES

1   What is the shape of Low Lorton in grid square 1525?
2   Describe the site of Buttermere.

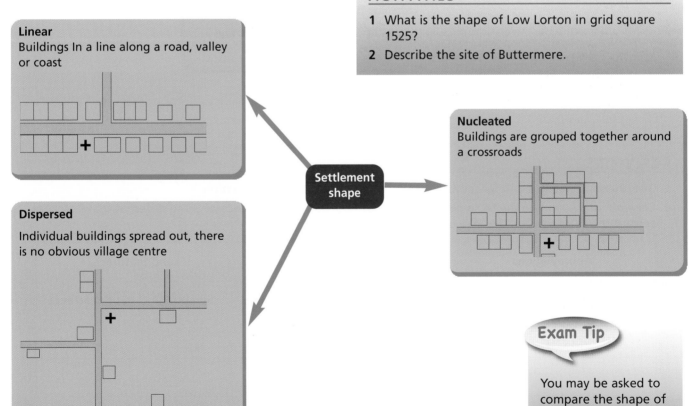

Linear
Buildings In a line along a road, valley or coast

Settlement shape

Nucleated
Buildings are grouped together around a crossroads

Dispersed
Individual buildings spread out, there is no obvious village centre

Exam Tip

You may be asked to compare the shape of two settlements on a map.

Human activity from map evidence

Maps show a large amount of human activity; most of it can be identified by looking at the key. You could be asked to use the information to produce sketch maps or questions relating to the distribution of different features.

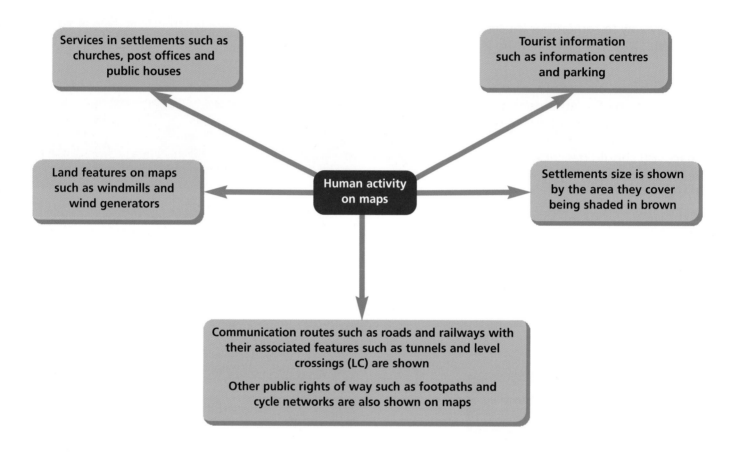

ACTIVITIES

1 Give the six-figure grid references of five different types of tourist information.
2 Copy out and complete the table below with the symbol and grid reference of three different features from each of the categories on the map key.

Abbreviations		Communications		Land features	
Symbol	Grid reference	Symbol	Grid reference	Symbol	Grid reference

Use maps with photographs, sketches and written directions

Many exam papers have questions that require you to be able to use the OS map with a photograph. This will mean you need to orientate the photograph with the map. The top of the map is always north – you must turn the photograph looking for important features until the photograph is pointing in the same direction as the map.

Figure 7

 Exam Tips

The types of questions you could be asked are:

- Recognition of certain features which have been identified by a letter on the photograph.
- The direction the photograph was taken.
- A comparison of features that can be seen on the map and not on the photograph and vice versa.
- The grid reference of the location of where the photograph was taken.
- Use the OS map to complete a sketch.
- There may also be questions which ask you to give directions from one place to another or to follow directions identifying features that you pass along the way.
- You could also be asked to identify sketche best route between two places.

ACTIVITIES

Figure 7 was taken at grid reference 168150.

1 Name the two bodies of water (lakes) labelled A and B on the photograph.

2 What is the height of the hill at point C?

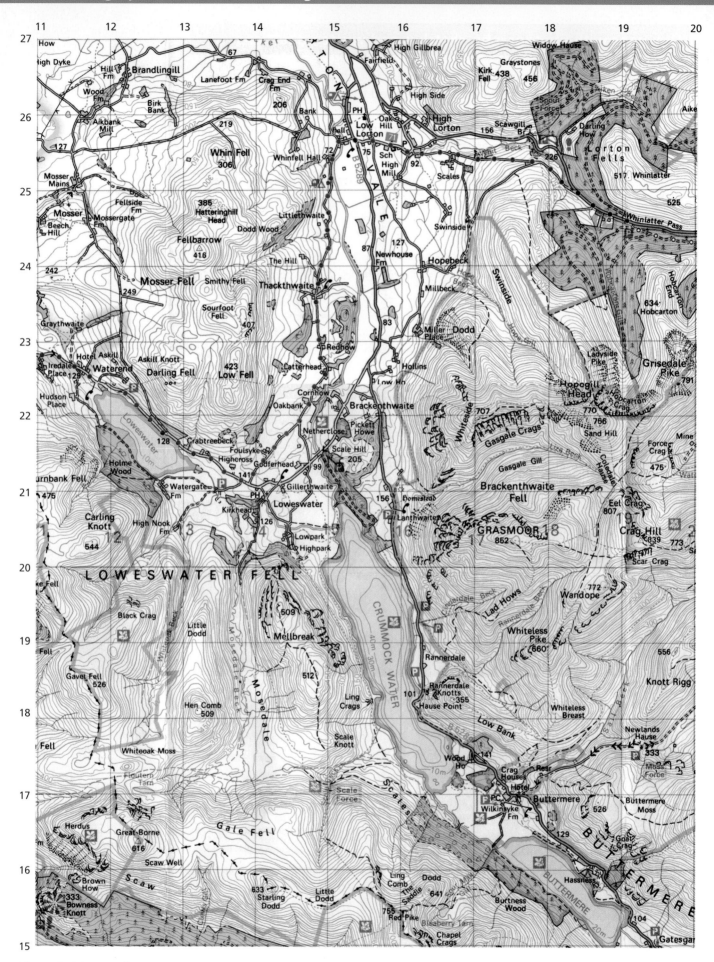

Figure 8 OS map of Loweswater

3   Graphical Skills

The exam specification states that:

● you will need to be able to construct and complete a variety of graphs, charts and maps

● you will need to be able to interpret a variety of graphs, including those located on maps and topological diagrams.

The graphs listed below are the ones that you will be expected to know how to construct, complete and interpret. Some of the graphs are constructed in a similar way. So, how are your graphical techniques?

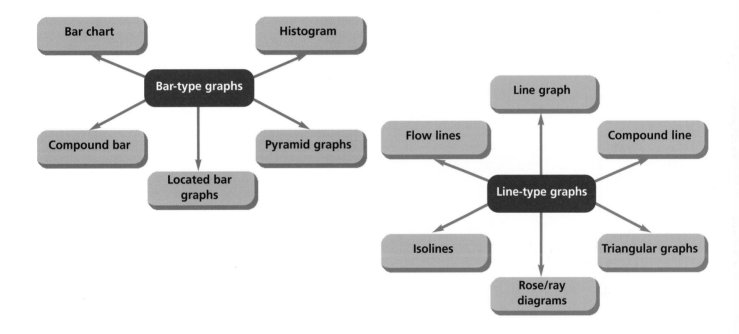

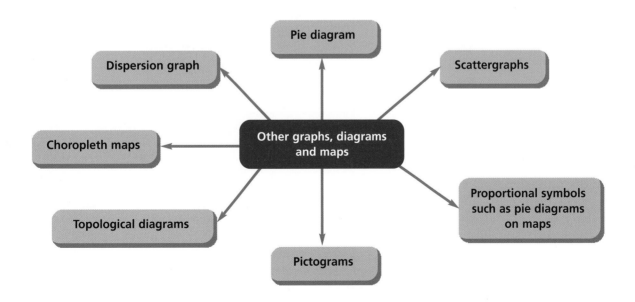

Bar-type graphs

Some of these will be very familiar to you, bar charts and histograms are examples. The difference between these is that a **bar chart** is used to display discrete (non-continuous) data and a **histogram** is used to display continuous data.

Bar charts and histograms can be drawn horizontally or vertically, the length of the column determining how many of the items are being displayed.

Other bar graphs are more difficult, such as compound bar graphs and bar graphs that are located on maps. A compound bar graph has a number of different pieces of information in each column. It could be just one column or have a number of columns, such as in Figure 1. This graph shows different employment sectors in a number of countries. By using a compound graph for this data, the differences between the countries can be seen easily.

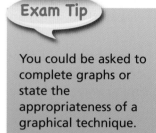

Exam Tip

You could be asked to complete graphs or state the appropriateness of a graphical technique.

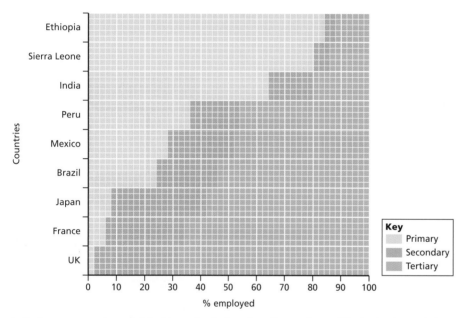

Figure 1 A compound or divided bar chart showing the sectors of industry in certain countries

ACTIVITY

Describe the differences between the selected countries' sectors of employment.

The compound bar graph shown in Figure 2 has been drawn with a gap between the areas that the data is being displayed for. This makes it easy to read the information. However, the patterns are easier to recognise if there is no gap between the bars.

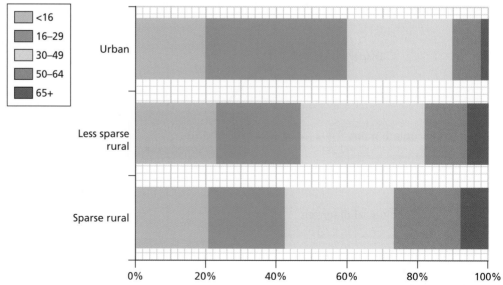

Figure 2 A compound bar graph showing age groups of people in urban and rural areas

Pyramid graphs

The usual form of pyramid graphs is a population pyramid as shown in Figure 3. You could be asked to complete the graph or you could be asked to interpret the graph. You would not be expected to give reasons for the changes that you state.

Bar graphs can also be located on to maps such as Figure 4. You will be expected to be able to construct bars on maps and to be able to interpret them.

ACTIVITIES

Draw two sketch pyramids which represent the pyramids in Figure 3. Interpret the pyramids by labelling them with the following information:

● women live longer than men
● a narrow base shows a low birth rate
● wide bands at the top show a low death rate
● fewer baby girls than boys
● few older people indicating a high death rate
● wide base shows a large number of children
● more elderly women than men; women live longer
● high death rate shown by steps in bars.

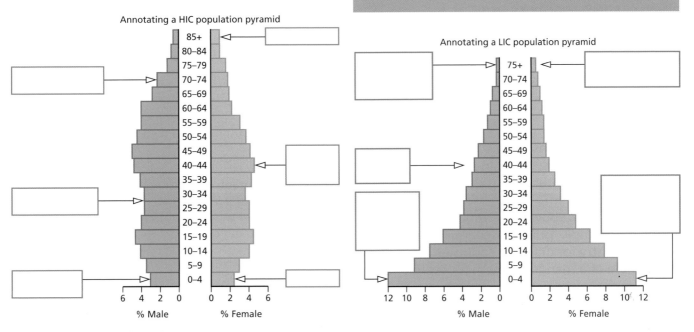

Figure 3 Two pyramid graphs

Exam Tip

You could be asked to interpret the information portrayed by a graph or diagram.

ACTIVITY

Describe the pattern of carbon emissions shown in Figure 4.

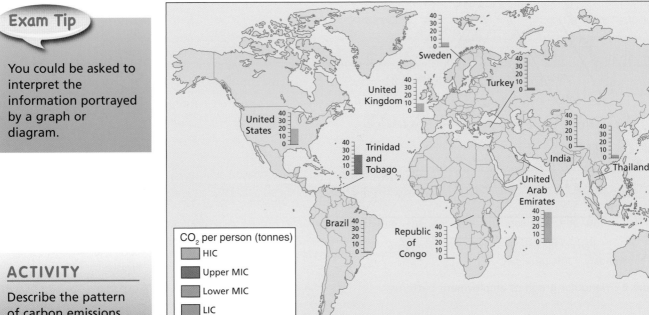

Figure 4 Carbon emissions for selected countries

Line-type graphs

Line graphs are used to show data that is continuous. An example is Figure 5 which shows China's gross domestic product (GDP) from 1950 to 2005. The information is continuous because there is not a break in the years. Other types of line graphs are flow lines and isolines.

Flow lines are usually used to display some kind of movement such as pedestrian or traffic flows over time. Isolines are lines which join places which are equal, for example, contours which join places of equal height and isovels which join places of equal velocity in a river.

Ray or rose diagrams tend to be used to show the direction of movement of groups of people. The length of the arrow would be the number of people and the arrow direction shows where the people come from.

Compound line graphs show continuous data for a number of variables; they can be some of the hardest graphs to interpret.

Triangular graphs show three variables on one graph, for example, primary, secondary and tertiary industry for different countries. Figure 6 is an example of a triangular graph for sectors of employment.

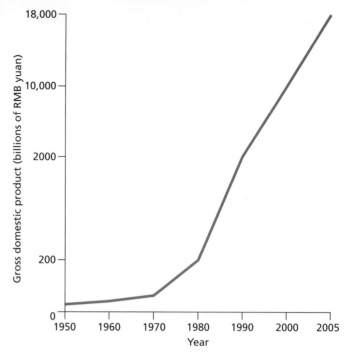

Figure 5 China's GDP 1950–2005

ACTIVITY

Why is a line graph an appropriate way to display the data in Figure 5?

Exam Tip

You could be asked to recommend the best type of graph to be used for a particular piece of data.

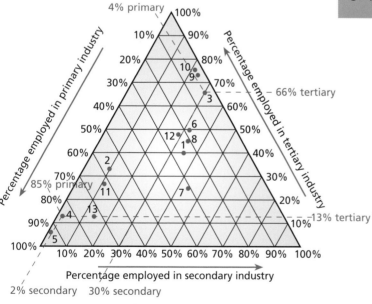

Figure 6 Triangular graph of employment patterns

ACTIVITY

Describe the sectors of industry of the countries shown in Figure 6.

Other graphs, diagrams and maps

Pie diagrams and pictograms

A pie diagram, or divided circle, is a graphical technique for showing a quantity which can be divided into parts. Pie diagrams can be located on maps to show variations in the composition of a geographical phenomenon. A pictogram is a way of portraying data using appropriate symbols or diagrams which are drawn to scale, as shown in Figure 7.

Another way of portraying data is proportional symbols on maps. These are usually circles but can also be squares or even symbols. The circles on Figure 8 are drawn to scale to portray the information on renewable energy.

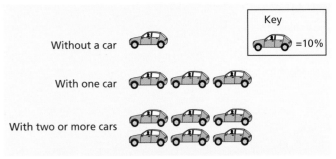

Figure 7 Car ownership for people living in a village

Exam Tip

You could be asked the advantages and disadvantages of a particular type of graphical technique.

Scatter graphs

Scatter graphs show if there is any correlation between two sets of data. The correlation can be positive: as one set of data increases so does the other set of data; or negative: as one set decreases, the other set decreases.

Dispersion graphs, choropleth maps and topological diagrams

Dispersion graphs show the range of a set of data. Choropleth maps show data over an area. On topological diagrams, the position of the place remains the same but the distance and direction are not so important.

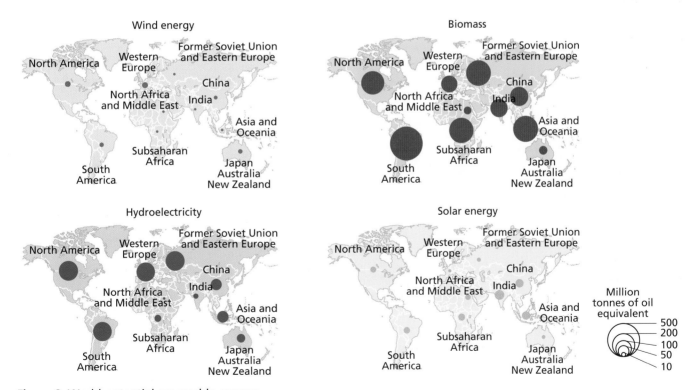

Figure 8 World potential renewable energy

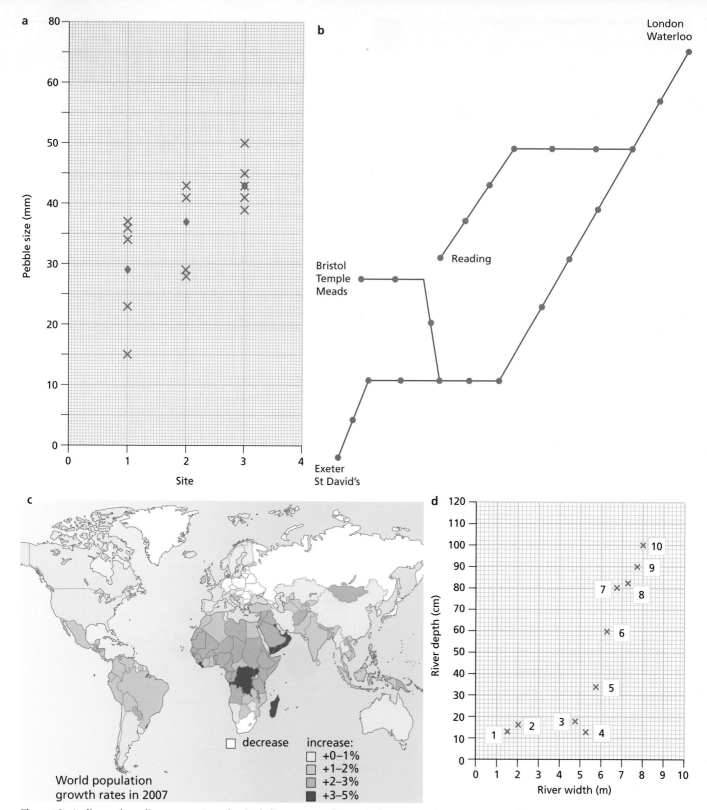

Figure 9 A dispersion diagram, a topological diagram, a choropleth map and a scatter graph

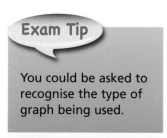
ACTIVITIES

1 Copy and complete the table for Figure 9. Put a, b, c, d in the correct place in the table.

2 Justify your answer to part 1.

Type of display technique	
Topological	
Choropleth	
Scatter graph	
Dispersion	

Geographical enquiry skills

There are a number of geographical enquiry skills which you could be examined on in the Unit 1 paper.

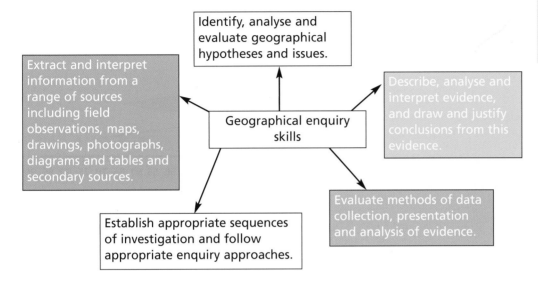

Identify, analyse and evaluate geographical hypotheses and issues.

Extract and interpret information from a range of sources including field observations, maps, drawings, photographs, diagrams and tables and secondary sources.

Geographical enquiry skills

Describe, analyse and interpret evidence, and draw and justify conclusions from this evidence.

Establish appropriate sequences of investigation and follow appropriate enquiry approaches.

Evaluate methods of data collection, presentation and analysis of evidence.

Exam Tip

Geographical enquiry skills will also be tested on Unit 4, Investigating Geography.

Some of these skills are more likely to be examined than others.

Extract and interpret information from a range of sources including field observations, maps, drawings, photographs, diagrams and tables and secondary sources

For example, study the map of the River Thames drainage basin. Here a map is used and information has to be extracted from it.

1 Which River flows through Luton?

2 The River Thames flows from point X and point Y. Name three cities that the River Thames flows through.

3 Which city does the River Thames flow through first?

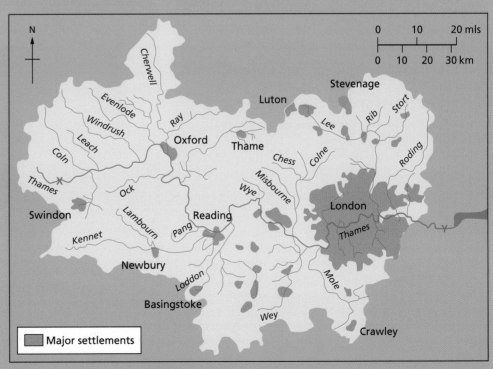

Describe, analyse and interpret evidence, and draw and justify conclusions from this evidence

For example, study the pedestrian counts completed at different locations in Windsor, Berkshire.

1   Describe the information shown on the graph.

2   Suggest reasons for the patterns shown by the data.

3   What conclusions can be drawn from this information about the various locations in Windsor?

Here questions are asked about pedestrian flows recorded at different locations in Windsor. First, the evidence is described; the second question asks for some interpretion of the evidence; the third question asks for concluding comments.

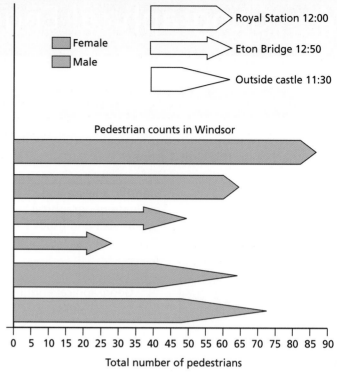

Evaluate methods of data collection, presentation and analysis of evidence

Study the choropleth map of which county most visitors came from to Lulworth Cove in May 2007.

1   Suggest reasons why a choropleth map is a suitable technique to display this type of information.

2   Suggest one other technique that could have been used. Explain why it is a more appropriate technique than a choropleth map.

Here the questions evaluate a data-presentation technique. Other questions could ask you to evaluate methods of data collection or the analysis of evidence. However, these are less likely to be asked.

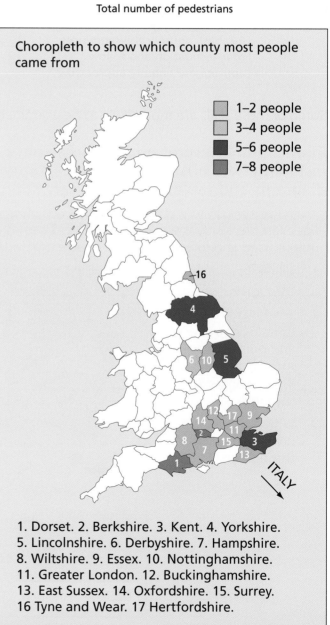

Choropleth to show which county most people came from

1. Dorset. 2. Berkshire. 3. Kent. 4. Yorkshire.
5. Lincolnshire. 6. Derbyshire. 7. Hampshire.
8. Wiltshire. 9. Essex. 10. Nottinghamshire.
11. Greater London. 12. Buckinghamshire.
13. East Sussex. 14. Oxfordshire. 15. Surrey.
16 Tyne and Wear. 17 Hertfordshire.

ICT skills

There are a number of ICT skills which are listed in the exam specification.

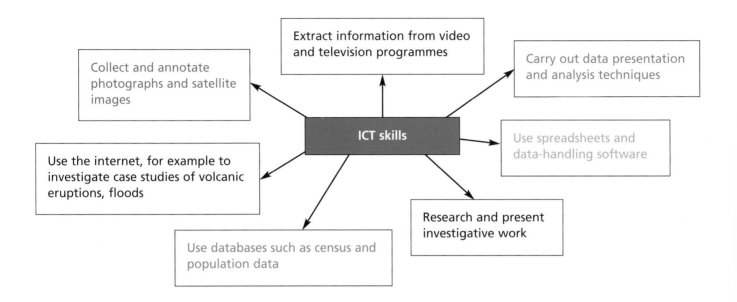

It is unlikely, but some of these skills may be examined on Unit 1:

- use the internet, for example, to investigate case studies of volcanic eruptions or floods
- extract information from video and television programmes
- research and present investigative work
- use spreadsheets and data-handling software.

Use databases such as census and population data
You could be asked to interpret census data. This could be in the form of a database.

Exam Tip

Collect and annotate photographs and satellite images
You would not be able to collect photographs for the exam but you could be asked to annotate a photograph using information from a piece of stimulus material or perhaps the OS map.

Exam Tip

Carry out data presentation and analysis techniques
For this you could be asked to complete a graph such as a bar graph or a map such as a choropleth map. You could also be asked to carry out data analysis techniques such as a scatter graph.

5 Geographical Information System (GIS) Skills

Geographical Information System (GIS) skills

You must have knowledge of the workings of GIS.

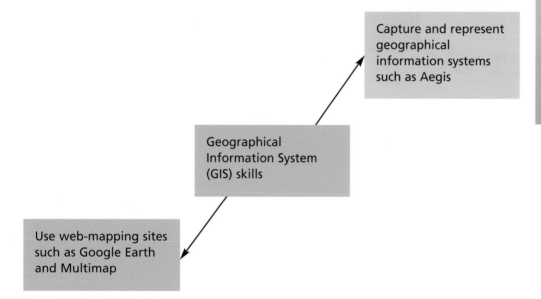

Capture and represent geographical information systems such as Aegis

Geographical Information System (GIS) skills

Use web-mapping sites such as Google Earth and Multimap

There are a number of ways that GIS could be examined on Unit 1. You won't be asked to go to the computer room and capture information or use a web-mapping site, but there are lots of questions that might come up.

- What is GIS?
- Who uses GIS?
- What is layering?
- How is GIS used?
- How can GIS improve data presentation?
- What are the advantages and disadvantages of GIS?
- How do web-mapping sites work?
- How have you used GIS?

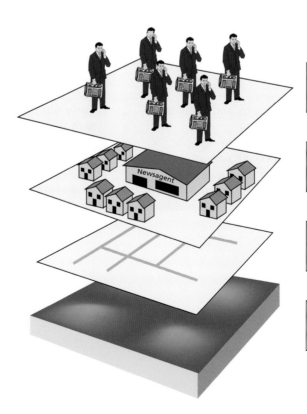

The people indicate where newspapers are delivered to each day.

This layer shows houses. The central building is a newsagent.

This layer shows the roads of the area.

Base map showing physical features.

ACTIVITY

Try answering the questions in the box above.

6 Challenges for the Planet

The causes, effects and responses to climate change

How has the world's climate changed since the last ice age?

The temperature over the last 10,000 years has increased by 6°C. However, there has been a number of fluctuations in this general trend.

Between 4000 and 8000 years ago there were two warm periods interrupted by a colder spell.

Another warm spell happened between 1500BC and AD1200, part of this period was known as the medieval warm period.

The temperature is projected to increase much more rapidly in the coming years, being 5°C warmer in 2100 than it is now.

After the last ice age, the temperature rose rapidly for the following 1200 years.

In the past 100 years the temperature has begun to rise steadily, with greater increases since the 1960s.

Between AD1250 and 1850 the temperature remained cooler. This was known as the little ice age.

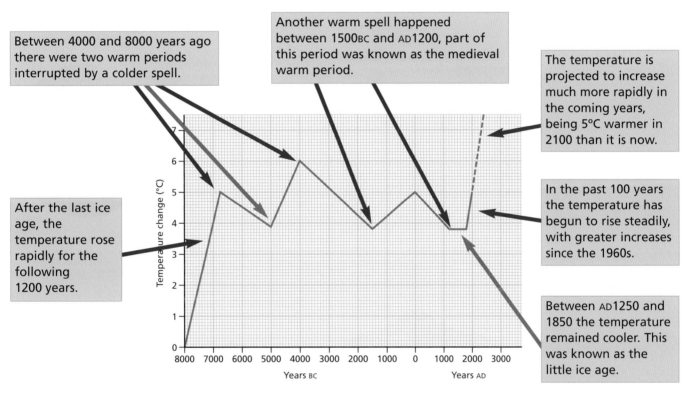

Figure 1 A graph of the world's temperature since 8000BC

The world's temperature has increased over the last 10,000 years by 6°C.

This is a general point.

The temperatures rose steadily between 8000BC and 7200BC.

This is a specific point.

ACTIVITY

Describe how the world's climate has changed since the last ice age.

Exam Tip

Remember that when you are describing a graph you should start with the general and then make specific points.

Why has the world's climate changed since the last ice age?

Figure 2 The factors that affect the world's climate

This is energy that comes from the Sun. Measurements made in the 1980s showed that the total amount of solar energy reaching the Earth has decreased by 0.1 per cent. If this continues, global temperatures could start to decrease between 0.5 and 1°C.

It is thought that the activity of sunspots on the Sun's surface affects solar output. There was a period of drastically reduced sunspot activity between 1645 and 1715 which might have been one of the causes of the little ice age.

External factors

World's climate

Solar output

Internal factors

Volcanic activity

Surface reflection

Volcanic eruptions release large amounts of sulphur dioxide and ash into the atmosphere. These act as a cloak and reduce the amount of solar (radiation) energy reaching the Earth's surface. In 1815, Mount Tambora erupted. The following year was unusually cold over much of the world with Europe having heavy snowfalls and frost throughout the summer; 1816 became known as 'the year without a summer'.

During cooler periods when there is a larger amount of snow and ice on the Earth, global temperature will drop due to the snow and ice reflecting sunlight back to space. As the planet starts to warm up, snow and ice will diminish, and the Earth will continue to get warmer.

The tilt of the Earth's axis varies over time. This variation occurs over a 41,000-year time period. When the angle is greater, the Earth usually experiences warmer periods.

The Earth's orbit around the Sun varies from nearly circular to elliptical and back to circular again every 95,000 years. There are many conflicting views on what happens to temperatures as the Earth's orbit's shape changes. Cold, glacial periods seem to have occurred when the Earth's orbit is circular and warmer periods when it is more elliptical.

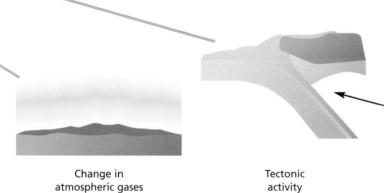

Orbital geometry

Change in atmospheric gases

Tectonic activity

The movement of continents caused by plate tectonics affects the global pattern of atmospheric and ocean circulation; and the changing shape of the Earth's surface causes winds and ocean currents to change.

ACTIVITY

Explain what is causing this decrease in solar output.

Clue – increase in car ownership!

There is a clear relationship between the amount of carbon dioxide (CO_2) in the atmosphere and temperature variations. Carbon dioxide is one of the most important gases responsible for the greenhouse effect. The greenhouse effect keeps heat within the Earth's atmosphere by absorbing long wavelength radiation. Without the greenhouse effect the average global temperature of the Earth would be –18°C rather than the present 15°C.

ACTIVITY

Find out what a sunspot is.

The causes of current climate change on a local and global scale

Climate change has a number of different causes; these include the burning of fossil fuels and the increase of methane in the atmosphere.

Fossil fuels

When fossil fuels such as coal, oil and natural gas are burnt they produce carbon dioxide which contributes to the greenhouse effect causing climate to change. There has been an increase in the burning of fossil fuels to produce energy in countries such as China where 75 per cent of energy is produced from coal. China is developing rapidly and using coal to fuel this development. There has been an increase in global car ownership which has caused an increase in the use of oil, which in turn increases the amount of carbon dioxide in the atmosphere. Drilling for oil also releases methane in the form of natural gas.

Methane

Methane makes up 20 per cent of the greenhouse gases in the atmosphere and is 20 times more potent than carbon dioxide. The amount of methane in the atmosphere has risen by 1.5 per cent a year for the past decade. But why?

- There has been an increase in bacteria emissions from wetlands because of rising temperatures.
- There has been an increase in the growing of rice because of the increasing population in rice-producing countries. Rice is grown in marshy conditions.
- There has been an increase in the number of cattle for meat reflecting an increase in Western-style diets. Cattle produce methane as they ruminate their food.

Figure 3 The Norfolk Broads – a wetland area

Figure 4 Rice growing in a paddy field in Sri Lanka

Figure 5 Cows ruminating in a field in Devon

Exam Tip

When the command word **compare** is used, you should state the similarities between the photographs or figures that have been given. However, examiners at GCSE will also credit comments about the differences (contrasts).

ACTIVITIES

The land uses in Figures 3–5 show three causes of current climate change. Explain how these land uses cause the climate to change.

The negative effects of climate change

Climate change has negative effects on the environment and people. These negative effects can be at both a local and a global scale. On a global scale there has been a change in crop yields, sea levels and glaciers.

Melting ice in the Arctic could cause the Gulf Stream to be diverted further south. This will lead to colder temperatures in western Europe, matching the temperatures found across the Atlantic in Labrador at the present time. Temperatures are frequently below 0°C in the winter with averages of 8–10°C in July, which is 10°C cooler than the average UK summer temperature.

Glacier National Park, Montana, USA was created in 1910. At this time there were 150 glaciers. Since then the number has decreased to 30. It is predicted that within 30 years most if not all of the park's glaciers will disappear.

In the UK, different crops can be grown such as bananas, due to rising temperatures.

Research published in 2007 by the Met Office's Hadley Centre for Climate Change, showed that between 1993 and 2006 sea levels rose 3.3 mm a year. This will lead to an 88 cm rise in sea levels by the end of the century.

Rising sea levels will threaten large areas of low-lying coastal land including major world cities such as London.

Tanzania and Mozambique will have longer periods of drought and shorter growing seasons. They could lose almost a third of their maize crop.

Figure 6 The negative effects of climate change

Research has shown that 90 per cent of the glaciers in Antarctica are retreating.

In Kenya, droughts now happen every 3 years instead of every 10 years. In 2006 Kenya suffered its worst drought for 80 years. Many farmers lost all of their cattle.

There has been a loss of sea ice due to climate change. This is a problem for polar bears of Wrangel Island, a Russian nature reserve, because they cannot travel overland to catch their prey.

Bangladesh suffers from coastal flooding. Experts say if the sea level goes up by 1 m, Bangladesh will lose 17.5 per cent of its land.

Two of the Kiribati islands are now covered with the sea.

Due to rising sea levels, Tuvalu (a group of nine coral atolls in the Pacific Ocean) has started to evacuate its population to New Zealand, with 75 people moving away each year.

In India there will be a 50 per cent decrease in the amount of land available to grow wheat. This is due to hotter and drier weather.

ACTIVITY

Explain the negative effects of climate change. Use examples in your answer.

The responses to climate change – from a global to a local scale

Global scale responses

Global agreements between nations

- **June 1992 – The Earth Summit, Rio de Janeiro, Brazil**

  This was a meeting organised by the United Nations to discuss climate change. The result of the meeting was the first international environmental treaty which aimed to stabilise greenhouse gas emissions.

- **December 1997 – Kyoto Conference, Japan**

  At this meeting the Kyoto Protocol was signed which came into force in February 2005. By 2008, 181 countries had signed the Kyoto Protocol.

  The agreement's main points were:

  - Greenhouse gas emissions to be cut by 5.2 per cent compared to 1990 levels globally.

  - Each country agreed to a national limit on emissions which ranged from 8 per cent for the EU, 7 per cent for the USA, 6 per cent for Japan and 0 per cent for Russia.

  - It allowed increases of 10 per cent for Iceland and 8 per cent for Australia because they were not using all of their carbon allowance.

  - In order to achieve their targets, countries could either cut their emissions or trade with other countries in carbon. This means that a country could buy carbon credits from another country. For example, Iceland could trade 2 per cent of its carbon credits with the EU to enable the EU to meet its target of 8 per cent.

- **December 2007 – Bali Conference, Indonesia**

  Representatives of over 180 countries were present. The result of the meeting was the Bali Roadmap in which initiatives were agreed to try to reach a secure future climate.

Exam Tip

If the command word is **outline** you *should* describe in detail. You should not make any explanatory points but if you do 'slip' into explanation your work will be credited.

The actions of non-governmental organisations

Greenpeace is focusing its campaign against climate change on the use of fossil fuels. It is trying to get governments, especially the UK government, to change their policies so that energy is produced in a more sustainable way.

They have a number of ideas:

- A lot of energy is wasted when it is being produced, for example approximately two-thirds is lost in waste heat in cooling towers. If this waste heat was captured, the amount of fuel needed to produce energy would be reduced.

- Energy is also wasted because of the distance it travels from the power station to houses where it is used. One way to save energy would be to use combined heat and power systems. These produce energy for a small area and therefore the energy travels a shorter distance between where it is produced and where it is used.

- If energy is produced using renewable sources this would further reduce the use of fossil fuels. The UK is building many offshore wind farms to supply some of its energy needs.

- Transport produces 22 per cent of the UK's carbon emissions. Low carbon or electric cars need to be produced and public transport made more efficient.

- Air traffic produces even more of the UK's carbon emissions than cars. If the government restricted the number of airports to be built and raised taxes on flights to make them more expensive, this would perhaps reduce carbon emissions.

ACTIVITY

Outline the responses to climate change on a global scale.

Local scale responses

By schools

'Live Simply' is a campaign which ran throughout the whole of 2007. It was initiated by the Catholic Church to encourage students to consider how they make choices in life. It provided a number of resources for schools which made students think about their impact on the world and sustainability.

Many schools are introducing energy-efficient water and central heating systems run from renewable sources such as wind turbines or solar panels. Schools also have reminder notices to switch off lights.

Twenty-five school wind turbine projects in England, Wales and Northern Ireland, have been funded by The Clear Skies scheme. By the time the initiative comes to an end, £12.5 million will have been allocated to education projects since 2003.

By local companies

The wind turbine at Green Park in Reading has been providing energy for 1500 homes and businesses since 2005.

Figure 7 Green Park in Reading

By local interest groups

One such group is 'Manchester is my Planet'. This group is running a 'pledge campaign' to encourage individuals to reduce their carbon footprints and become involved in a number of green energy projects. The group started in 2005 and works with the local council. There are now over 20,000 people who have pledged to work towards a low-carbon future. One of the initiatives is the Green Badge Parking Permit. People who own low-carbon emission cars can apply for a permit that allows them to have discounted parking in the city.

By local councils

The UK government believes that local councils are important in the reduction of carbon emissions as they have an influence on local homeowners: 15 per cent of the UK's carbon emissions are produced by houses. The government has given local councils £4 million to help them to develop ideas which will cut carbon emissions. Woking Borough Council has used the money to provide power to some of its public buildings, see Figures 8 and 9.

Figure 8 Woking Park Leisure Centre

Figure 9 Vyne Community Centre and Knaphills Surgery, Woking

ACTIVITY

Describe the responses to climate change on a local scale.

If the command word is **describe** you should state the main characteristics.

Sustainable development for the planet

Definitions and interpretations of sustainable development

In 1980 the United Nations released the Brundtland report which defined sustainable development as:

> 'Development which meets the needs of the present without compromising the ability of future generations to meet their own needs.'

A key area of sustainable development is that it should not hinder development, but give a better quality of life both now and in the future. In the UK four key sustainable areas have been identified:

- **Climate change and energy** – reducing greenhouse gas emissions in the UK and worldwide while at the same time preparing for the climate change that cannot be avoided.
- **Natural resources** – the limits of the natural resources that sustain life, such as water, air and soil, are understood so that they can be used most efficiently.
- **Sustainable communities** – places that people live and work in need to be looked after by implementing ideas such as ecotowns and green energy.
- **Sustainable consumption and production** – the ways that products are designed, produced, used and disposed of should be carefully controlled.

The development of policies by large organisations to make them more sustainable

Large organisations have realised that they must be more sustainable. They can achieve this in many different ways:

- during the manufacturing of the product
- in the recycling of packaging material
- by encouraging customers to recycle products
- by encouraging employees to be more sustainable in the workplace.

ACTIVITY

Define the term sustainable development.

The food industry – Asda/Walmart

Asda's distribution centre in Didcot, Oxfordshire, now recycles all of its plastic packaging rather than sending it to be disposed of in a landfill site.

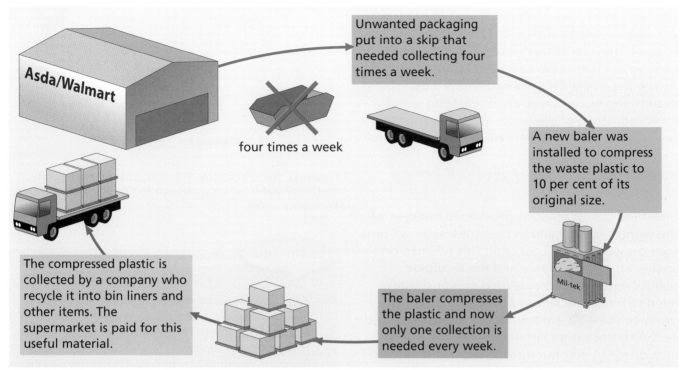

Unwanted packaging put into a skip that needed collecting four times a week.

four times a week

A new baler was installed to compress the waste plastic to 10 per cent of its original size.

Mil-tek

The compressed plastic is collected by a company who recycle it into bin liners and other items. The supermarket is paid for this useful material.

The baler compresses the plastic and now only one collection is needed every week.

Figure 10 A supermarket's approach to reducing landfill by recycling by using a baler to compress waste plastic

Asda benefits because it is paid for the plastic which is recycled. The environment benefits because plastic isn't sent to landfill sites.

The communications industry – Nokia

Nokia are concerned that people do not recycle their old mobiles. If every mobile phone user recycled one phone it would save 240,000 tonnes of raw materials. Nokia gives information on its website on where to find recycling points and the address to send the phone to if there is not a centre nearby.

Over 50 per cent of mobile phone users change their phone every year.

44 per cent of these old phones are left in drawers at home.

100 per cent of the phone can be recycled.

Old mobiles can be used in the manufacture of trumpets, park benches or even gold rings.

Figure 11 Mobiles about to be recycled

A global company – General Electric

General Electric is a large transnational corporation (TNC) which operates in many different countries. It is trying to manufacture its products in a more sustainable way. Water is a valuable resource, and by 2012 General Electric hopes to reduce its freshwater usage by 20 per cent, which is enough to fill 3000 Olympic-sized swimming pools. This will be achieved by monitoring water usage and improving water recycling. Much of the water in the organisation's boilers and cooling towers will be recycled water.

Power generation – coal-fired power stations

Coal-fired power stations provide 38 per cent of the world's energy and in countries such as China they provide over 75 per cent. This reliance on coal as an energy source and the resultant pollution means that coal-fired power stations need to be as efficient as possible in order to produce the least amount of pollution. Coal-fired power stations emit large amounts of carbon dioxide (CO_2), sulphur dioxide (SO_2) and nitrous oxide (N_2O). These gases are major contributors to both acid rain and climate change. Figure 13 shows ways that the emissions of these gases are being reduced.

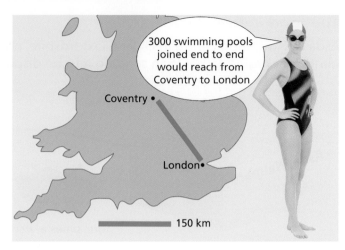

> 3000 swimming pools joined end to end would reach from Coventry to London

Coventry •

London•

150 km

Figure 12 General Electric wants to save 7.4 million cubic metres of water, which is enough to fill 3000 Olympic-sized swimming pools

Exam Tips

- You could be asked questions that require recall of knowledge. You should learn specific points about the policies of large organisations to make them more sustainable.
- Read the question carefully and don't get caught out.

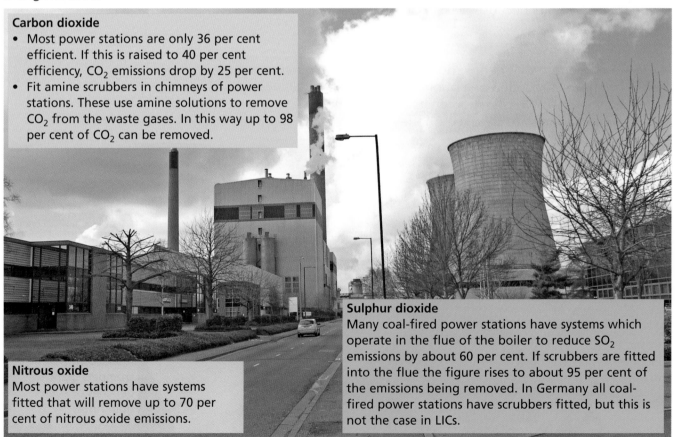

Carbon dioxide
- Most power stations are only 36 per cent efficient. If this is raised to 40 per cent efficiency, CO_2 emissions drop by 25 per cent.
- Fit amine scrubbers in chimneys of power stations. These use amine solutions to remove CO_2 from the waste gases. In this way up to 98 per cent of CO_2 can be removed.

Nitrous oxide
Most power stations have systems fitted that will remove up to 70 per cent of nitrous oxide emissions.

Sulphur dioxide
Many coal-fired power stations have systems which operate in the flue of the boiler to reduce SO_2 emissions by about 60 per cent. If scrubbers are fitted into the flue the figure rises to about 95 per cent of the emissions being removed. In Germany all coal-fired power stations have scrubbers fitted, but this is not the case in LICs.

Figure 13 A biomass power station in Slough

Figure 14 Sustainability in the workplace

Schools often have separate waste bins for paper and card in their classrooms. Pupils are also encouraged by signs to switch off lights. Most schools also have their computers controlled centrally so that a piece of software switches all the computers off and on in the school at set times.

The use of video conferencing reduces a company's carbon footprint.

Hotel companies have a policy of only washing towels if the clients ask them to, therefore reducing water usage and soap powder.

The internet (email) is being used more to send information and documents. This means that less paper is being used. Many companies aim to become paperless in the future.

Large companies provide their employees with a variety of different bins to deal with waste products. There are not only bins for waste paper but also for other types of waste. Other ways to introduce sustainability in the workplace include notices to switch off lights and push taps in toilets to conserve water.

Tourist destinations provide a variety of ways to recycle waste.

Sustainable development in Dartmoor National Park.

The management of transport in urban areas

Sustainable transport involves maintaining the standard of transport that is required for society and the economy to function efficiently without placing too much pressure on the environment.

In urban areas of the world, there is a great dependency on the car as a means of transport. In both HICs and LICs people are becoming ever more dependent on private vehicles for moving around the city. Car ownership is growing most rapidly in LICs and MICs. In Delhi, India, the number of vehicles in the city has grown from half a million in 1970 to over five million in 2008.

Governments want people to give up using their cars and travel on public transport more frequently. The problem is that the car drivers will not use public transport until it is cheaper and more efficient.

There are two ways to manage traffic in urban areas:

- Respond to the increasing demand by building more roads. This might help congestion but will eventually lead to even more vehicles and an increase in pollution levels.
- Reduce traffic with a range of sustainable schemes. A wide range of sustainable transport schemes have been introduced around the world to alleviate the problems of congestion and pollution.

Sustainable transport schemes

There are a range of sustainable transport schemes which can be used, including:

- Car sharing, where workers share lifts to work using their own cars. If half of UK motorists received a lift one day a week, vehicle congestion and pollution would be reduced by 10 per cent, and traffic jams by 20 per cent.
- Designated cycle and walking paths within the urban area. Milton Keynes is one of the best served urban areas in the UK with 273 km of cycle paths.
- Road lanes that only allow cars with at least two passengers to use them. There is a designated two people lane close to a university in Bristol.
- Road lanes that give priority to buses, ensuring they get an easy passage through congested areas. There is a designated bus lane from the A329M directly into the centre of Reading.

ACTIVITY

What is meant by the public versus the private debate?

ACTIVITY

List all the specific points you can remember about the Cambridge park and ride scheme and the congestion charge in London.

Congestion charging

- Congestion charging is a scheme for making motorists pay to travel into large urban areas during periods of heaviest use. The aim is to reduce the number of vehicles entering the city which will ease traffic congestion and therefore lower pollution. It will hopefully lead to more sustainable forms of transport like walking, cycling or public transport being used.
- The first place to introduce a congestion charge was Singapore. Motorists in Singapore have been charged to go into the central city area since 1974. The first city in the UK to introduce congestion

charging was Durham. The Durham Road User Charge Zone is located in the centre of the city – it includes Durham Cathedral and Castle, as well as Durham Market Place, Durham Chorister School, Durham University colleges and a variety of shops and businesses. It operates from 10.00a.m. until 4.00p.m., Monday to Saturday. The £2 charge is paid on exit.
- A number of other cities have now introduced congestion charging zones including London, Oslo and Stockholm.

London congestion charge

- London introduced the congestion charge in 2003 at which time it was £5. It is based on a system of cameras that photograph and then register car licence plate numbers in its database. These cameras are located at all entry points into the congestion charge zone and within the zone itself and actually photograph both front and rear plates on entry and exit of the zones. It operates from 7.00a.m. until 6.00p.m., Monday to Friday. On 5 July 2005 the change was increased to £8.
- In 2007 the congestion area was extended but that extension was removed in January 2011, at the same time the price of the original zone increased to £10.
- By 2008 it had had the following beneficial effects:
  - Traffic levels have been reduced by 21 per cent.
  - 65,000 fewer car journeys a day.
  - An increase of 29,000 bus passengers entering the zone during the morning peak rush period.
  - There has been a 12 per cent increase in cycle journeys within the zone.
  - There has been a 12 per cent reduction in the emission of nitrous oxide and fine particulates.

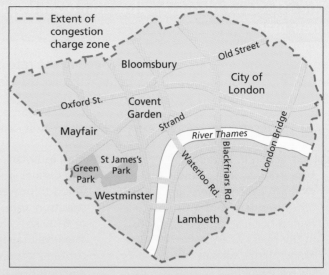

Figure 15 The congestion charge zone in London

Park and ride

Park and ride schemes allow shoppers to park their cars in large designated parking areas on the edge of the urban area and catch a bus into the town centre. Parking is free but there is often a charge for bus travel to the city centre. The park and ride sites are usually located on the main routes coming into the urban area, so they are easily accessible for the greatest number of car users. Approximately 40 people will travel on one bus rather than in 40 individual vehicles, which means there will be much less congestion and pollution.

Cambridge park and ride

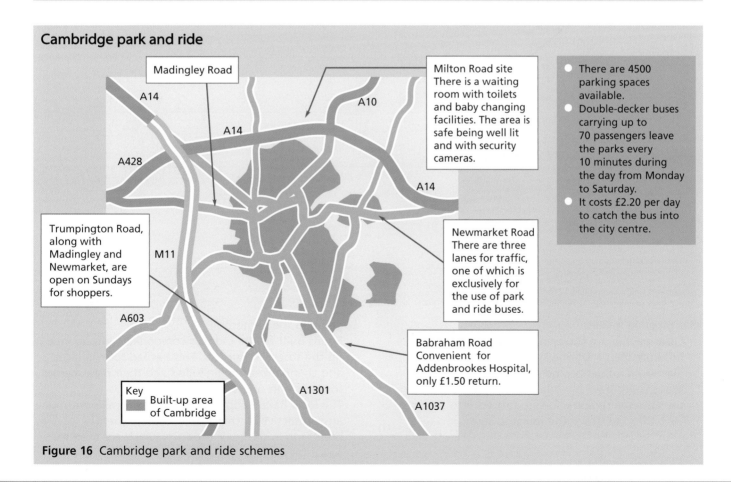

Figure 16 Cambridge park and ride schemes

The effects of resource extraction from tropical rainforests and their management

Tropical rainforests are being destroyed at the rate of 32,000 hectares per day. The size of the remaining forest is about 5 per cent of the world's land surface. Much of the area which remains has felt the impact of human activities and does not contain its original biodiversity.

Figure 17 The effect of resource extraction from tropical rainforest

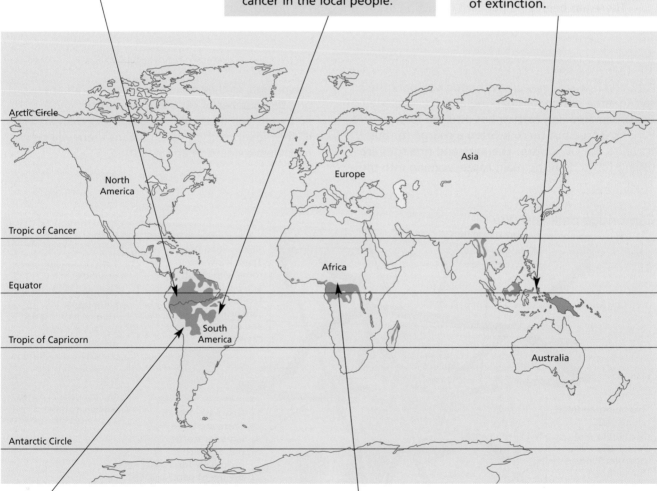

Oil extraction in Ecuador
- Miscarriages are common and stomach cancer is five times more frequent in the Oriente region because of hydrocarbons in the river water.
- Many plants, such as the periwinkle which is used to cure childhood leukaemia, are becoming extinct.

Mining in Brazil
- The Carajas iron ore plant uses wood to power the plant. This results in annual deforestation of 6100 km².
- The River Tapajos is contaminated with mercury used when gold is mined, affecting 90 per cent of all fish caught. This leads to high levels of cancer in the local people.

Mining in Indonesia
- 285,000 tonnes of mining waste are dumped into the River Aghawaghon every day. This pollutes fish and means there is a shortage of water for local people.
- Crocodiles in the area of Teluk Etna are currently on the brink of extinction.

Gas pipeline in Peru
- Local people are exposed to diseases that they are not immune to. During the 1980s half of the Nahua died from influenza and whooping cough.
- Many roads have been built through the forest in the Camisea region allowing settlers into the area who then cut down the forest to farm.

Logging in the Cameroon
- Roads built by the logging companies have opened up the forest to hunters. This has led to elephants and chimpanzees being killed and their meat being sold for high prices to restaurants.
- The local Baka people work in the sawmills without any protective clothing. This leads to them breathing in the toxic products which are used to treat the wood.

Tropical rainforest management

Figure 18 Tropical rainforest management

Ecuador
Oil has been extracted from the Amazon rainforest in Ecuador since the 1960s. The companies have done very little to manage the effects of the extraction. Recently the local indigenous people have taken the oil companies to court because of the destruction of their environment.

Texaco has agreed to pay $40 million to cover its share for cleanup of, among other things, some 160 of the 600 waste pits created. But the chief of the local Secoya tribe stated that $6 billion was needed to do the job properly.

Venezuela
Since 2008 the government of Venezuela has not issued any further permits to mine gold or diamonds in the Imataca Rainforest Reserve or anywhere else in the country. The country does not need to exploit the minerals for economic reasons (due to its oil reserves), therefore it can afford to conserve its forest area.

Madagascar
In 2001 Givaudan, a Swiss company, sent a team to Madagascar to survey for new fragrances. It developed 40 aromas that were then sold. The company shared the profits with local communities through conservation and development initiatives.

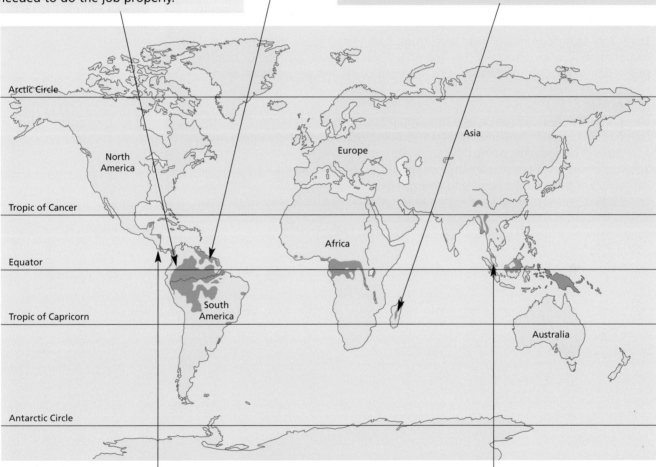

Costa Rica
Costa Rica is developing its rainforest in a sustainable way. One of the ways is through ecotourism. Many areas of the country, including the famous Cloud Forest area have developed tourist facilities such as zip wiring and trails through the forest which are very popular with tourists.

Malaysia
In Malaysia the government has rejected plans to build a coal-fired power plant at Silam, on the island of Borneo. The government decided that it did not want to pollute the area and more environmentally friendly forms of energy would need to be found.

The country has vast reserves of coal and other minerals such as gold. The government will not develop these resources at the expense of the rainforest which has many endangered species such as the orang-utan. Instead it is going to develop ecotourism, emphasising the natural attractions such as world-class diving and the biologically diverse tropical rainforest.

ACTIVITIES

Construct two tables or spidergrams. The first should contain all the information on the effects of resource extraction on the tropical rainforest. The second should contain the information on tropical rainforest management.

Exam Tip

Case study questions will use the following mark scheme:

Foundation Tier
Level 1 (1–2) A simple answer which has very little description. Could be about anywhere not linked to any particular study.
Level 2 (3–4) A basic answer with level two being reached by there being descriptive points or a specific point or possibly a weak explanation.
The top of the level requires a specific point and some linked descriptive points. Or a specific point and weak explanation.
Level 3 (5–6) A clear answer with level three being reached by there being a clear explanation or a specific point. The top of the level requires a range of specific points or a number of explanations or a specific point and an explanation.

Higher Tier
Level 1 (1–2) A basic answer which has simple descriptive statements.
Level 2 (3–4) A clear answer with level two being reached by there being an explanation or a specific point.
The top of the level requires a range of specific points or a number of explanations or a specific point and an explanation.
Level 3 (5–6) An explicit answer with a range of specific and explained points.

Exam Tip

Remember there are **two** topics to learn for the tropical rainforest:

1 The effects of resource extraction on the tropical rainforest.
2 The management of the tropical rainforest environment.

Higher Tier learn **three** examples for each.
Foundation Tier learn **one** example for each.